Prayers to a Small Stone

Prayers to
a Small Stone

Poems

Jo Brachman

Cider Press Review
San Diego

Cider Press Review
PO BOX 33384
San Diego, CA, USA
ciderpressreview.com

First edition
10 9 8 7 6 5 4 3 2 1 0

ISBN: 9781930781665
Library of Congress Control Number: 2024947334
Cover image: "Medicago Arborea," from *Seeds – Time Capsules of Life*,
photographer Rob Kesseler, courtesy Academy Editions Ltd
Book design by Caron Andregg

Winner of the 2023 *Cider Press Review* Book Award:
CIDERPRESSREVIEW.COM/BOOKAWARD.

Printed in the United States of America
at Bookmobile in Minneapolis, MN USA.

To the person with whom I've shared lifetimes: thank you for your love, your attention, and your support. To the many amazing adventures we've experienced that occurred due to your unbounded and uplifting spirit— this is for you Dave, my love.

Acknowledgements & Thanks

Grateful acknowledgment is made to the editors of the following journals and anthology in which these poems or earlier versions of them appeared:

Bellingham Review: "In the Air"

Birmingham Poetry Review: "Up Moons Grove Road"

Cimarron Review: "The Scientist's Hypothesis of Distance," "Upon Reading That Scientists Have Observed the Golden Ratio in Human Skulls," "Weeding Out My Mother's Photos"

Comstock Review: "What I Worry About in the ER"

Cortland Review: "Reprieve"

Hiram Poetry Review: "Things I Worry About While Driving Alone," "The Dental Appointment"

Moon City Review: "Suspended," "I say goodbye wraparound, but linger," "Matriarch," "What I Worry About at the Aquarium"

Poet Lore: "Native Medicine," "Second Death"

Poetry East: "Having Blouses Altered"

San Pedro River Review: "Busboy and Waitress at Everybody's Pizza," "The Desk" (appeared originally as "Office"), "Gulf of Mexico, Midnight Walk," "Trial Separation," "Before We Are Too Old," "Night-Mother," "The Shaman"

Spoon River Poetry Review: "The Mouth of the Pelican is Open"

SWWIM: "The Scientist and Her Husband Observed the Consciousness of Gnats in Spoleto, Italy"

Tar River Poetry: "Pencils," "Lessons," "The Artist on her Daily Devotional," "The Shaman Says Release"

Town Creek Poetry: "The Universe Continues to Expand at 6 a.m."

Valparaiso Poetry Review: "Letter Home," "Whatever the History Between Us," "Adoption, Second Day"

Waccamaw: A Journal of Contemporary Poetry: "Still Breathing"

"The Scientist's Hypothesis of Distance" also appeared in *Best New Poets: 50 Poems from Emerging Writers,* Samovar Press, chosen by poet and guest editor Mary Szybist.

Gratitude to the workshop teachers, participants, and retreats where some of these poems were born, built, or read: Callanwolde Fine Arts Center, West Ga. University, Writersbloc, Poetry @ Tech, The Hambidge Center, and Good Bones Group. And to my Pacific University MFA program mentors: Dorianne Laux, Ellen Bass, Kwame Dawes, Frank X. Gaspar, and Joe Millar.

Also, much gratitude for the many that provided laughter, insight, and groundedness along the way: Jackie, Kim, Mary, Melanie, Lisa, Kelly, Kay, Coco, Margaret, Allison, Amy, Stevie, Jen, Memye, Will, Emily, Carla, Carol, Nancy, Michele, Maudi, Pam M., Pam D., Martha, Mindy, Laura S., Keitha, Zander & Raya, Annie, Sarah & Steve, Sarah P., Laura & Tom, Philip & Ronnie, Bob & Michele, Katie & Travis, Elisa, Emanuela, Daniela & Gianluca, Daria, Emily & Justin.

To my siblings: Katie, Fred, Steve, and Zack.

And forever a special thanks to Katie Chaple for her skillful shepherding.

Many thanks to Caron Andregg, Catherine Campbell, and judge Jayne Marek, for choosing my manuscript for the Cider Press Review Book Award and for transforming it into a reality.

To my talented son, Alexander; your insight into human nature never ceases to amaze.

Contents

III

IV

V

1

On foot
I had to walk through the solar systems,
before I found the first thread of my red dress.
Already, I sense myself.
Somewhere in space hangs my heart,
sparks fly from it, shaking the air,
to other reckless hearts.

—Edith Södergran (1892-1923)
(tr. by Stina Katchadourian)

Busboy and Waitress at Everybody's Pizza

Outside behind the dumpster, speed
in his coffee, he swallows the metallic night.
Revving the engine inside, the bartender

cranks up "Statesboro Blues." A winning soccer
team zings coasters. One server yells,
Lady with a baby, coming through, shoulders

the crowd blocking the aisles. Full throttle,
eight hours of sauce-smeared trays, coins
of pepperoni and silver anchovies caked

on sneakers. At a backroom booth she lays down
her tip apron, douses a cig in the last customer's
swill. He lays down his dirty rag,

and best pick-up line of the night, tells her
for lovers' breath, they both must eat onions
if they're going to kiss. They reek the same

sweat, and at her place, shower off
what they've earned, sleep until the next shift.
Every night different, every night the same—

if it weren't for the lonely, if it weren't
for a jaded stench welling up, if it were not
for people, they could love everybody.

In the Air

On the porch we shake the dead
lightbulb day and hear broken filament
in our voices. You ask, *Are you listening to me?*
How can I answer—*No.* My silence orbits
the yard, the circling makes us suffer.
Long ago we pledged an oath: no poisons.
But toxins infest—rashes of *you shoulds*
settle on the crowded magnolia.
We were younger when we dug that hole,
unaware how large the blueprint of limbs.
Thunder shatters at the roof tin,
shakes through the leaves
all loosened things letting go.
We move through the house closing windows,
meet midway in the narrow hall.
Say it first. Say you love me.

The Universe Continues to Expand at 6 a.m.

Standing under a faded sky,
what you are feeling,
whatever you have tried not to feel,
arrives. You begin mourning
like an ancient, as if you remember
a pre-dawn more star-filled.
Bright flash gone missing,
the sky withers down
on all towns of the earth,
their bodies of water reflecting
kitchens with people devoted
to explosions of their present
moment. Monstrous beauty escaping,
the sky burns up
dark edges of the trees.
Gravity lets go
what you had hoped to keep.
Your body numbs as if you are the space
in-between,
as if you have already gone.

I say goodbye wrap-around, but linger

on the wicker with our dog. I say goodbye
house-ghost. She's the sad, haunted one,
but when I leave, she must stay.

I say goodbye kitchen stinking
of marigolds, red mailbox twined
with purple clematis. Goodbye back stoop,
tin roof, chimney's crumbling brick.

I wave to the blurred conductor shaking
this crossroad town. I should wait. I should say
goodbye dear husband,
tell you how the long nights shook

the moon from the leaves, breathed
life backward from the trees,
how for hours I tried to divine an escape.
The train's faint signal droned: *Dead summer,*
raise up your thin limbs and go.

Trial Separation

What if I'd said, *I'm staying*
and instead of the luggage in my car,

I see the small grove of pecan trees
dropping their bounty in our yard.

What if my body lets go all its untold sorrow.
Our dog's tail could wag.

And my hand could find the soft spot
between his ears. Not the frown,

the worried whine that I'm leaving him
behind, not the pacing of an animal that knows.

Here I make my bed, and everything
around the cabin is dying.

All I can think to do is drink alone
at the window, watch the leaves fall, and listen

to the thinning maples, their trunks—
bars straight and quiet.

Through the woods at the primate center,
an electrified fence. The apes burst

into the outdoor compound, break
the silence at feeding time, bark out

decrees stark as prayer. Who will kiss
their wild hands goodnight? Shave

their granite chests, tattoo a number?
Who will wake them? Who wakes you,

and how will I wake myself
when trapped in runaway dreams?

In this interim forest, I worry
a male will breach the barbed wire

on bare-breasted nights when I no longer recognize
myself in the mirror. He stalks me at the open

bedroom window, sticks a fist through—
his leathered palm, his fingers uncurling.

Still Breathing

Lately, I'm afraid of not living
close enough to the seeded
circle of wild flowers,
but out the window
I see the purple bergamot
has jumped the rock border
nearer the dogwood
tree where bees mumble
the hummingbird feeder.
One bee squeezed into the red
plastic flower and spins in the sugar
water, its wet furry body
trembles up to a pocket
of breath, drunk and not knowing
there is no escape from heaven.

Things I Worry About While Driving Alone

Eighty flat miles, and I worry I won't remember
how to go home. I'll forget to read my map,
to stop for gas and snacks. The zapping sun
between flanks of pines will blind me.
A dusty side trail will pull me in like a dark mouth,
the steering wheel turning on its own volition,
tires eating a weedy path straight to a broken-down trailer,
where, sitting in sweaty boxer shorts, seven burly men
burp beer clichés, talking about how no means yes,
how any woman who would venture down the dead end
to their squalid door, not only would be lost, but loose.

I worry the car lock my husband did not repair
betrays me. Pulled out, hoisted in air,
I'm a jostled testosterone trophy.
The men fight over me. I am the last
fried drumstick on the plate,
their last remnant of hen.
The most bravado wins. He has a tender side, his chest
abloom with fragile stars. We fall in love.
I cook venison stew for all, send the other six packing,
estrogen the place until it sparkles.

I worry I am never found.
I worry my husband won't miss me.
I worry my husband will miss me.

Letter Home

—Piazza del Campo

If they ask, tell them about the hotel—a medieval tower
that distorted acoustics, and from the lobby,

a morning sneeze spiraled up fifty steps to my door.
That the owner pouted each time she remembered

I travelled alone. If they ask what I saw, tell them
a short walk opened into a huge piazza where students

slept on stone, and backpacks and bellies served as pillows.
Children blew bubbles. Men hawked umbrellas.

And reigning above it all, a she-wolf
statue suckled twin boys. If they ask what I heard,

tell them a man reminded me of you,
his eyes closed to the sky making love to his violin.

Say among the thousands in Siena, I eavesdropped
on an Italian couple arguing in the crowd,

as if it all came down to this defining moment,
forcing a sea of moving tourists to part around them,

then come together again. I wanted to wave a wand over
their rising voices. If they ask how different night

was from day, say at night I bolted the shutters
against thunder. Tell them the ceiling made of tree trunk

and pitted bricks rumbled. And as the sky let loose,
I let go a sadness and a joy I had pulled too tight,

and I cried with abandon. If they ask,
tell them dawn was clear-eyed like a Roman sun

pouring wash buckets onto cobbled alleys.
Tell them outside my window across tiers of rooflines,

pigeons wrestled insects from moss on the clay tiles,
a dawning palette rang in a day of mottled gray.

The Scientist's Hypothesis of Distance

Blue nothing. She considered miles
out the high window in the stairwell.
First, simple paper-distances her finger

could trace, point A to point B.
Then more difficult measurement,
that of closeness, like bonded atoms.

And then, hypothetical expanses
like those of the heart's vessels—
their length could circle the globe twice.

A plane seemed to crawl across the glass,
leaving a necklace vapor trail. She believed
in possibilities, that every atom that could exist,

already did, but still, she could not wear the red
strapless dress she no longer owned,
couldn't lift her hair for his fingertips to clasp

pearls at the nape of her neck, his breath
fastening a shiver between her shoulder blades
down the small dip of her back.

She wanted to look into a large aperture
telescope, to view the farthest reaches
of visible space, where no energy had ever been

destroyed, to see into the incalculable vastness
of him in their living room downstairs, him
on the brown sofa reading. She wanted

him to put down his book, to think of her
on the landing, waiting. For him to move
exponentially faster, up the stairs two at a time.

Pencils

Your sweet joke, Husband: box after box.
I sharpened the dull, graphite eyes,
arranged in mason jars, vases, retired
coffee cups. Stand-up-straight harbingers
bloomed in every corner of our house,
contained all words ever invented,
their nipple-colored erasers not yet worn
to nubs by too many blunders.
I never mentioned what I discovered:
the leadless anomaly. Or the one I found
on your desk after our fight,
its yellow length riddled in teeth marks.
Or the one with the perfect point for drawing
a love note—stick figures with private
thought bubbles above our heads.
In all, a thousand number 2 pencils,
more than enough to last years.
We were patient and knew
it would take time to hone something
that would not break under pressure.

Lessons

Is this what it means to be human—
light from an endless sky
filling you with hope and sadness?
You'd been trying to think
about dark matter again,
each time feeling like you're nothing
but the tiniest vein in a giant's
forehead that throbs with a headache
when she stands up and hits
the ceiling. Like trying to learn
Italian, your brain stuffed with love
letters written in disappearing ink.
Your language teacher said
Learn the verbs not like an American,
but like an Italian. She said
they never say, *Memorize by heart.*
Instead, they use the head to store
essere or not *essere* in the brain's
warehouse of labeled boxes.
For now, you leave the cosmos
and other conjugations.
You give that pulsing mystery
of the heart a rest too, its ardent muscle
never built to bear weight or hold
indefinitely. Its job: to send forth,
to take back, to beat,
and if the owner is lucky,
occasionally, to skip.

Déjà Vu in the Spoleto Archeological Museum

Diggers pried a greenstone axe,
pots forged black, wine set
for twelve thirsty dead—

artifacts the grave could not confine—
all cleaned, classified, encased
behind glass in a deserted museum.

We amble among the remains.
It feels like a past we already know,
so vast we could slip inside it,

as if the objects' stories have always
been a part of our own. Maybe you
were a woman then, maybe I was

a man, or we were both men
or women. I stop to consider the teeth
of a comb whittled from bone.

You pull me to you. We kiss the kind
of kiss in movies—the kind when a couple ignites,
rushes into an apartment, and slams

against a wall, proving science wrong:
objects are solid. But they can't wait
to prove science right—boundary

is pretense. And we know they'll burn through
the space between each other's molecules,
nothing will stop them becoming permeable.

Isn't that what the body craves?
To taste passion formed inside,
to leap past the impediment of language,

the sediment of thought? Our blush feels new.
(Or is it old?) I sense something or someone
watching us from a lit shelf—a small country

of bronze statues only an inch high, familiar
as if cast by our own hands—genderless
Etruscans with arms spread wide.
Welcome back.

The Scientist Thinks About Mystery

We are stardust,
We are billion-year-old carbon

—*Joni Mitchell*

Take this night. And the underbelly of things.
Take the body. We want to believe we know

ourselves and that we know each other,
even though we inhabit a domain

we don't understand. Take the sweet breath
of your own essence—your molecules skimming

the lake of my neck. I run my hand
along the contour of your uncountable acres

between unstoppable atoms.
The throat's concave pocket, its secrets

never meant to be turned inside out.
Take us, in our skin—the dark underground

of my palm resting on your chest, the bone cage
underneath that protects your lungs

and holds the heart I can't hold in my hands.
And even if I could, its electric impulse

to beat would remain unseen.
Take the matrix beneath the nails,

or the mouth's anchor-hinge,
the spit-glitter underworld of the tongue.

Take the forgetting sex brings, lost
to all sensation, save us. Take it all.

Take none of it. On earth, the future pools
in marooned shoes, but dust endures,

folds under its own invisible attraction.
In another galaxy, a new presence, a star,
how it peels away sweat from our tangled legs.

Before We Are Too Old

The sun will feed us,
    maybe not like that time
    in the orchard when we pulled
    off our clothes, and bees
    churned inside rotting apples
    as we rolled on the quilt.
But here too, the sky slips through
    interstices of green clouds.
Come visit me. Climb the stairs
    to a prism full of books,
    comfortable chairs, light.
Leaf orbits dangle
    with squirrels. And a red blur—
    a pileated woodpecker's head
    hammers up a limb.
A daring feat, but not if you consider
    planets in balance never rotate
    too slowly to be pulled in by the sun,
    nor too fast to pull away.
You may be interested to know my body
    is separating from its younger one.
    Sometimes I forget I have a body,
    but its ache reminds me.
You and I are cadavers-in-training,
    we ride this ball into deep space
    alongside other galaxies,
    pulled toward the *Great Attractor.*
Sometimes I feel like I forgot
    to live my life.
Climb the stairs. Come visit me.

The Scientist and Her Husband Observed the Consciousness of Gnats in Spoleto, Italy

Nothing but a blur of brevity. She saw it first.
He tried to capture it—lens-click—still a cloud

of nothing. They'd been sitting on the wall outside
the duomo at early dusk, talking about spending

their last stage of life in a foreign country. To die
here, where the light of the old masters' brushes

washed the stucco, the cobblestones, their faces.
The small flies arrived. Each frenzied gnat created

the larger, slower shape of a moon in-the-making.
The males moved as swarms do—with one mind

to attract females who would only join
the churning mass to mate. The mundane

ghost-bodies spun, wings backlit by the sun's
last bone-colors of the ancient.

The gnats would live for hours, at the most
a few days, coded to cheat death by breeding.

The couple vowed to be reborn for a chance
of another lifetime together in this fortress town

where long ago, Etruscans divined the future
by gazing into a goat's liver. The two watched

in silence. Rising above the duomo piazza,
the flies swelled into a thousand prayers.

Latitude and Longitude

We could be anywhere
to exist, but we've traveled
half-way round the world.
You snore with the pleasure
of the revived dead,
while Italian words splash
against stone in delayed dark—
a couple walking past
our apartment, their sky divining
lost umbrellas and rain.
After years of planning
the future, last night we found
ourselves alive in the only place
we could have—the present.
A blanket on the couch,
slow light comes in curves
naming each object.
I sip hot tea. Oh, to crawl
inside you and listen
where talk in dream-tongue
bears no translation.
I make coffee, but the aroma
doesn't rouse, not yet.
I study my palm. I've forgotten
what these arching paths predict,
discard the noise of the past—
signs and omens of fortune-tellers.
It's morning, and I'm awash
in the invisible
and imaginary straight lines
that take us directly to each other,

ready again to create the new
that will disappear as soon
as we've created it.
Wake up lover-turned-
mapmaker-of-distances.
Come find me here
at the crossroads of this planet,
where all is measured
by the speed of thought,
and the real navigation
happens now, now, and now.

II

I'm ceded—I've stopped being Theirs—
The name They dropped upon my face
With water, in the country church
Is finished using, now,
And they can put it with my Dolls,
My childhood, and the string of spools,
I've finished threading—too—

—Emily Dickinson

Morning Radio Fly Me Away

Three feet from her parents' bed,
her father's hangover snores.
She waits for the music
that will take her from this room,
her metal bed against the bolted
fireplace smelling of coal.

Up the chute, rain has just begun
tinging the capped chimney.
The radio clicks on.
An orchestra brings Ginger Rogers
and Fred Astaire to steer the girl
across wooden floors, out and down
the front stoop, slender ankles
below twirling chiffon, tuxedo
tails flying. Both tap dancing
on a glistening street where umbrellas
spin, and the mountain range
of oak roots serves as a prop to jump on,
then pushing off from the trunk.
Along the weed-choked sidewalk,
seated violinists trill the strings.

The girl hurries to keep up,
grabs a handful of sequined hem.
Ginger stops and turns to look.
The girl holds tight, but her father's
cigarette cough begins the day,
muffled sounds of heavy
breathing under the parents' quilt.
She covers her ears with her hands.

Night-Mother

When the sleeping pill released her jaw,
when my mother rolled over
into the Night-Mother, it seemed like a hundred
years she'd been dreaming red-legged frogs,
mossy rocks coated with ocean salt.

She wore a nightgown the color
of that luna moth her fingertips
once peeled from our screened door.
When I asked, she said that frayed green
death-fluttering her palm
could not help itself—a drug-eyed beauty
craving light it could not reach.

I wanted to shake her awake,
but closed her Bible, the tissue-thin
promises underlined—how she taught me
to read two summers before—the book
she searched for escape paths to slip onto,
quiet and barefoot, past heart-shaped leaves,
faster where hill-trees shook
loose the last of winter.

I could not follow into high grass
where she slept with moaning
buffalo ghosts. No room at the edge
for me to curl into her softness.

I could not enter or endure
the empty side where my father's pillow
held smoke, the shape of his head,

and the oiled smell of his hair.
The sheet tangled in her dreams,
her arm and shoulder bare.
I tried to cover her.

I Forced My Mother to Laugh

Christmas of extremes.
My father wasn't home (I don't know why)
just that we could make noise
when I woke up to the world's largest
peppermint stick, the smallest tea set,
and a book that was not a book at all,
but a package of Lifesaver candies.

Then, a doll my size when I groped
her by the waist, each strand of her pretend
hair shiny, her dress in pink,
with lace-trimmed socks atop stiff
patent-leather shoes. I'd slept in my school
clothes (I don't know why)—
a plaid skirt and sweater.
My recently sheared hair stuck straight up.
You said like a rooster's. You said smile
for brother's camera. Kiss the plastic cheek.

I twirled with the big fake girl.
Robed and legs crossed, your body
slung back in the chair as if my hilarity
had pushed you. You covered
your mouth as you laughed.
The no-name doll with blinking lashes
and permanent smile and I—
around and around we went. Each spin
around the room more desperate than the last.

Matriarch

It takes a certain kind of woman
to keep shucking husks at the table,
distract her granddaughter with the art
of pulling silk, demonstrate how
to scrape the cobs with a dull knife
to produce the milkiest kernels, salt
and butter for the sweetest cream corn.

Any son-in-law can show up late
and drunk at the latched screened door,
can yell his daughter's name.
And when Grandmother yells back, *No,
you're not taking her,* he can bang
the door wide open, enter a blackout of rage.

But it takes a certain kind of woman
to reach for an empty cast iron skillet,
a certain kind of woman to not hesitate
to deliver one solid blow. Her verdict laid out
on a rose motif floor, linoleum blooms
the size of festooned cabbages.

Order in our maternal grandmother's kitchen.
Order among the refrigerator and sink,
and in the pot on the stove, order among
the roiling field peas steaming
the late afternoon windows.

The Future Self Speaks to the Child Self

Listen carefully and do what I say.
For a long time, you will not be safe.
You must always know where he is.
When he comes into the kitchen, shrink.
Stare at your bare feet, or the vinyl squares
running to the back door. When he leaves,
stand at the sink. Above it, there's a window
with an eyelet curtain, and each
opening always holds a circle of sky.

When he whistles, everyone will go to him.
It will hurt to see the people you love
obey like dogs. When you can, slip out
to the backyard. Lie with your face
close to the ground. See how the ants
follow each other up the grass into a shocking sun,
their weight barely tilting the blade.
Watch as they travel down the underside,
disappear into dark, then lift back into light.

One night a rat will fall from the attic hole
in your bedroom ceiling. You will call out
for Mother, but he will come to kill it
with a broom, its belly exposed. Do not cry,
or he'll pull you into their bed, all night
his heavy arm slung across your body,
his whiskey snores souring your own breath.

Listen, you'll visit this place again and again,
but know this, I'll be with you.
Soon, you will pray to a small stone.

Hide your talisman in the drawer of the hope chest.
Only when you are alone, take it out
and let it warm your palm. You will see
there are really two stones, one dull gray,
and the other a tiny mountain emerging
streaked with rivers the color of milk.

Listen, I promise, I'm coming to get you.

Suspended

When I see cotton panties strung like prayer
flags on the clothesline, crayon colors
for each day of a little girl's week,
I send up a thought for the girl
of my jackhammer youth,
who that first night at college forgot
her mother had sewn her name
into everything, thought the serenading boys
signaled a raid, and assumed the mind
she possessed was her own.
She tossed out a pair from the third-story
dorm window, not black lace, but new, heavy
cotton, not French cut, but hipster underpants,
her calling card, a surrender of fragile bravado
that first night on an Alabama campus.
The next day in the cafeteria, boys dangled
the pair, stretched the elastic, defined her shape.
She heard her name, afterwards, always
synonymous with the *Oh-no*-mistake,
like standing in front of every mirror in town
in ancient underwear, her feet
crammed into uncooperative heels,
her heart an obsessive suitcase packed tight
with important questions: *When can I go home?*
Who will talk to me about real things?
What if my mother dies too soon?
In her head, a grueling boxing match of voices
yelling at the ring, where it looked like there might
be a death at the end, and eventually, there was.

Weeding Out My Mother's Photos

Erase the memory of that chilled day,
of the long cashmere coat with a rope
of fur collar around her neck.

Erase the backdrop of her parents' house,
and the broom-swept dirt of the backyard
where she stood in polished heels.

I don't know what occasion demanded
her hair to be pinned in movie-star waves
that made her look older than fifteen.

I don't know how this image survived,
a note on the back, *Day I met my future
husband.*

       Erase the chickens,
the incongruous, doomed chickens—
one eyeing her, the others oblivious,

scavenger heads to the ground
like someone had tossed a handful
of grain seconds before the photographer

said, *Smile.* Her face lifted to what must
have been a cold sun, no hint
of the hurt she'd suffer,

cause, and allow. No sign
of the looming prison of a marriage.
Wait. Never erase this moment.

This girl still has time to believe
in herself. Here is the girl I can praise.
Maybe here was the mother I loved.

This morning, I want to sing a praise song,

but my tongue fattens with sugar and rust.

Once upon a time my mother handed me a dictionary
of silence. I became a silverfish, stripped

the threaded binding, sucked the glue, stuffed
my mouth—washed out not with soap, but blood

and whimsy. You ask why I try to offer my dead
mother a blessing, the whisper who taught me

and my paper doll how to read the red
promises of the Gospels—*the meek shall inherit.*

You say when she taught me letters, she
must've known how words silken into a testament,

she must've known how sentences collude
into a ball of rope that lead in, but also out

of my father's labyrinth. And my mother closed
her eyes lest she turn to salt.

And from the grocery store, a treat of cookies
from a circus wagon of caged animals. Some

with severed heads. I ate the damaged first.
And Little Golden Books of cats and birds

making a home. No teeth on neck, no chewed wing.
You say how odd to pair innocent animals

who cooked meals and washed dishes,
with St. Michael's brimstone steeds, to pair them

and his angels forcing the floodgate, crimson
down streets of gold. Up the marble steps,

her muted click of low Sunday heels. I'd behave
in church, or she'd still my kicking legs.

During prayer, the rattle of the mint wrapper fueled
the power of her eyes. To please, I'd swallow

the sacrament of grape juice, grind the store-brand saltine.
To please, I'd mouth the verse with the congregation,

I walk through the shadow. Mother, you admit,
that woman you were, must've known.

The child's body must have told. You say it's obvious
I loved the woman you were, but how?

This morning, I don't know how
to forgive, much less sing. I imagine you slipping

into your robe, the one with the pink swirls
of tufted flowers and spring-green stems. I imagine you

sun-drenched in a room of lowest heaven.
Is it true one can offer nothing to the dead

but volumes of the unspoken? I hand them to you.
Read. Then we can talk more. As a child, I was afraid

facts would break you or that you wouldn't believe,
which would have broken me. This morning, I'm telling

you my secrets. I'm opening the door.
Bless us both, bless us as sleepwalkers waking,

not broken but cracked open. For now, the two of us
forever cleaved apart, forever cleaved together.

III

*I came to see the damage that was done
and the treasures that prevail.*

—Adrienne Rich

Self-Portrait as Vulture

She plucked a feather's iridescence,
which reaped and reflected
what she becomes—wing, beak, air.
Above the wire, the ache
under her ribs stretches her claws.
She can't forget feeding at the wake
with others, a taste of wild decay
in her mouth. The group circles, but she floats
on the updraughts alone. Stolen vespers
from clotheslines, from lighthouses,
from fenceposts don't help her descend.
Tearing a path through desecrated grasses,
she searches for a nest below a carrion-colored sky,
abandons what is not hers to examine,
travels the miles, scans for signs in the waves,
studies the curved tongue and groove
along tree limbs. Clouds look like branches,
rooftops, cliffs—no place to land.
Her throat, a hollow reed of alarm.
Vision sharpens a thicket of dark rest,
and coming from a mile away the smell
of the fresh dead. Her third eye opens, closes,
opens. Perhaps she was wrong after all,
and hasn't flung her life across empty fields.

Having Blouses Altered

Seconds after we meet, I undress in front of you
and the noon weatherman on your 52-inch TV
in a corner of the living room workshop of buttons
and trim, sewing machines. Like a big sister
with good stories, you perform an emergency
airlift into a cheery distraction. Oh, let there be talk,
talk, and more talk in the house of the seamstress
with peach-colored hair, breath of peanut butter
lavished on vanilla wafers. You build beauty
queen dresses for five-year-olds with studded
rhinestones, key-lime crinoline swirls for that final
curtsy. Your ultimate creation hangs from the swag
lamp chain waiting to be worn by the next hopeful
Miss Toddler of Leon County, Florida: the costume
one wants to eat, once, if glutton for a sugar coma.
Pins in cushion, pins in mouth, you stick pins
under my arms, snug at my waist. I try on one blouse
after the next. Your chunky hands confident
at my hips spin me around to understand the curves.
Although taller, I lean like a little sister toward your
squat build. You promise what no therapist would:
I'm going to fix you right up. You'll see.
Now everything's going to fit better.

The Dental Appointment

Did I hurt you? the dentist asks, his nipples
waffle his tight uniform top. The room is cold.
I show him what I call my misbehaving tooth.

Turn up the magic, he says to the assistant,
and she does. In seconds I'm horizontal, hot
in the lamp's glare, dizzy in a nitrous haze.

His rubber glove cups my chin, an invitation.
Turn toward me and open wide.
And I do. *This may pinch a little.*

I'm going to rub it numb, and he does,
his breath on my cheek. He pulls on his mask,
and in his eyes, I see decades of teeth,

the clanking metal hook, his desire
to fix a stranger's ache, and for a second,
I want him to slip his married hands

into my married mouth
and pull each *Oh* from its hiding,
to ruin everything.

Whatever the History Between Us

I touch my mother-in-law's hands,
soft and cool as the tulip petals dropping
from the vase beside her chair,

small feminine hands that moved with hummingbird
speed across piano keys, that raised a fat cigar
to her lips, chin on shoulder striking an I'm-the-boss

pose recorded forever by the camera.
Rubbing my palms, I warm the lotion, begin kneading
the center of her palm, a deep push into the fatty pads.

That's what it is to begin to know the deeper ache.
She moans. I hold each finger at its base, pull down,
twist the thumb away from its meaty responsibilities.

I ease out the hurt lodged in the hinges,
the middle's wrinkled face, the knuckle's bony head.
I release the thirty-four muscles,

the twenty-seven bones, her hand limp and hanging
at the closed gate of her wrist.
She winces and whispers, *Wonderful,*

I don't want this to end.
And then I drape her hand over my fist,
a mortar and pestle, and grind her palm

as if I'm milling the pain into a fine powder
that I could simply blow away.

Wilderness the Body Has Entered

One dawn she wakes, twisted
idioms come tumbling down
behind her lids, a blue unraveling
alphabet she once owned.
Nothing follows.
Her jaw slack, a mask of teeth and lips.
We tighten our circle,
massage hands, prepare favorite foods,
but she is lost in fog, lost
in mirrors. Too late for her, nothing left
but seconds, untold hours,
even the mind's gnawing
worry-bone gone. Nothing that says
these are my legs, my hips, my breasts.
Lost to the body she lives in the gap
with no boundaries, no maps
no distinct roads, no signposts,
no name, no address.

The Artist on Her Daily Devotional

And I'm remembering the wonder.
Someone had given me a camellia
on a walk around the town's lake.
In spattered clothes, the painter
was out walking too, and stopped
as if seeing a flower for the first time,
blossoming right then from my palm—
deep pink, multi-layered, and the promise
of a tight bud in its center yet to unfold.
Do you want to paint it?
She looked at me and said, *No,*
but I could put it on my altar.
I've got an altar for God.
This god of hers so capital "G," so personal.
If the dead are going to speak
this would seem to be the moment.
Keep it, I said, already jealous. Maybe the dead
look at us and think, *Those poor people,*
they think their skin is a sealed envelope.
I wish my heart had been wide open.
I coveted the ease with which she could slip
far afield, sliding in and out beyond the borders.
The waking sky's white-gray clouds
knit a fog over the lake.

Cradlesong for My Future Child

I suspect he'll be a member of a secret tribe—
one of those children who stares
into mirrors until something stares back,
who navigates vast spaces without leaving home.
One of those children who hears the hum
of the underground, conjures the sap
rising on the leafed bough he sits on.
I wonder, when I call him, will it take a long time
for him to climb down, longer still
to slip back into his body.
I imagine him at night, listening to the tymbals
of the five-eyed cicadas, the net-veined throng.
A child who soaks in sound, and his torso
becomes the drum that ricochets
through summer's open windows.
I could see him sitting on a favorite rock,
or collecting small stones—rough and smooth—
kept in a box with a gold tassel.
I hope he doesn't think it's strange
to give names to his stones,
and that he'll make friends with others
who do the same, who carry talismans
in their pockets not for good luck,
but as a constant to warm their palms,
the ones who can sense the invisible,
and when strange days chant their psalms
of moonlight—like me, my child
will sometimes know a thing before it happens.

Adoption, Second Day

Your eight-month-old weight
on my chest tethered me to the bed.
Each time your tongue pushed against
your gums, I felt your jaw moving.
Like shards of some ancient Peruvian
lineage, buried teeth cutting through flesh.
Your throat vibrated, not like the future
morning, when you'd laugh outright,
but a purple-throated bird of late
afternoon pulsing my sternum with song.
Suddenly startled, quick flex of knees,
clenched hands. Followed by an exhale
of relief. Your nape muscles relaxed.
Your arms released their shield.
Vertebrae loosened, legs lengthened.
You became your true size.
A string of drool slid down your chin,
dampening my shirt. And as if you were mine,
my lips touched your fontanel, and I inhaled
your scent and inhaled your scent again,
and I wondered—in that other place
what had you heard, what had you seen?
I didn't even know your name,
but all this time the miraculous chamber
of your chest continued to pump blood
out to the edges of your ten fingers, ten toes.
And it came to me—you were becoming
mine, and I was becoming yours.
And all I had to do at that moment
was breathe, and listen to you breathe,
and you kept breathing.

What I Worry About at the Aquarium

For you, I want to love
the sea creatures,
the sideways eyes,
the quick movements,
the undulating grass,
but I worry they feel trapped.
Up against the glass,
I worry the enormous tank
will explode from their wild
sadness and longing for home.
It's been four years
since the court ruled
in our favor, and still I worry
if I'm not vigilant,
your biological parents
will snatch you from me.
We move along the corridor
behind a group of older kids.
I hold your small hand
too tight. You complain,
My hand is catching fire.
Instead, I hold on
to the back of your t-shirt.
You're stretching my shirt.
I worry my worry
will seep into you. I let go.
You dive into the noise
of the taller crowd.
You're suddenly up ahead,
and then nowhere.
Just when the panic

in my throat begins rising
to scream your name,
you emerge back at the glass
looking for me. We wave.
You dive again,
my slippery fish to watch.

Up Moons Grove Road

Midway up the mountain road, a stag held
dusk. I slowed the car to a halt.

Branching bones, cropped and copper fur,
flanks muscling off a fly.

I could not stop edging into dream, stunned
by the geography of hooves, the hollow clap

across the road to stand by pines—hymns
at the very top snapping blue in wind.

I could not stop unfurling as he turned to look,
his eyes quickening the blood in my neck

and arms. Down below, a truck
grinding gears. After, the buck, tail up,

in one jump became the wood.
Then I could not stop slipping into doeskin,

nosing among the hidden ferns.
But how to know myself rising off a bed

of bent weeds, velvet legs? How to lift
to smells of night and earth

up Moons Grove Road: the way back
home and steep climb out of her?

Prayer to a Green God

Spring again, and still,
others I love insist
on being dead,
even after the rainstorm
roused the fecund ground
into a museum of green.
I wonder at the curator-god
that again has poured canvas
green into Creeping Jenny,
happiness into asparagus.

Maybe this is the way
to second chances. Let me
love this world
as if it's the only one,
as if I'll pulse forever,
stretching across space
to become the infinite
awakeness of mint, bitter
bend of dandelion stem.

When I die, let someone
come looking for me
like I am looking now.
Watch my spirit hands
unfurl ferns—fishbone,
rabbit's foot, and bracken.

Let me become all the shades
of green, even the slime
and rotted muck of it—

the worm's iridescence,
the bloated frog
by the algae-covered fountain,
the muscled hearts
of metallic-green flies that sour
the mole's skull with larvae.
Let me join my present
and past loves singing in the dead
language—the music-throb-smell
of mowed wild onion.

Thoughts After No Sleep, Bailing Water Calf-Deep, Hauling Books to Higher Ground

The noisy geese after all night thunder-rain,
noisy geese wailing yet another language

she wants to know
because when they surge upward

with an urgent sound, their skein
weaves into a V, leaving the lake

a loud communion of warning.
It seems the geese know something

is coming with the vanishing dark
that has limped in a gray morning,

where the sunless lake swells
to meet the berm,

and another torrent begins.
And the old trees know too much

water will loosen the soil, that their heft
is always capable of cracking. The trunks

that only seem motionless can surprise
like a wrecking rod to smash

a house in two, flatten a car,
pull down a writhing power

that whips and sparks the streets.
And then how to recover?

How to piece back together what's left?
She wants to understand the forest

she read about, and a stump doomed
to rot that was rescued by neighboring trees—

their water messages rising through soil,
empathy busy underground making some new

thing that wasn't supposed to live,
but it does. And it keeps living.

IV

"Listen," says Kabir,
"I have a prayer to make.
I'm handcuffed to death.
Throw me the key."

—Kabir *(tr. Arvind Krishna Mehrotra)*

Gulf of Mexico, Midnight Walk

Brother, here is a benediction of the wild—
the grasses, the spiny burs, the sea-caked
sand pulling us tidal to the edge

where the infinite animal never stops.
I feel an excitement akin to fear
as we walk toward fallen stars—

shrimp boats blinking between
the two-grayed horizon.
Here is the immensity of the dark night,

the unfenced constellations rebirth us
as children trying to connect the dots
of the gods, hazy in penumbra shadows.

We resort to the comfort of old stories—
a flying horse born of bloodshed,
a Gorgon, and a demigod with a shield

who must kill what he dreads,
and without looking into her face,
or be turned to stone.

To the west the wind picks up,
our scarves flap back toward an east
with hours before the boats return.

The smell of the dying finds us,
each step a tug on our center of gravity.
The clouds shift. We stop and stare.

Here is the waning gibbous moon
announcing the terrifying *now*,
its cold light fanning out in our retinas.

What I Worry About in the ER

When the call comes, the news shocks
the kitchen clock, crushes the face
of my watch, shatters the air with a stillness

that makes me worry I'll be too late.
I arrive at the hospital in time, but you
don't know who I am. The broken hands

of the ER clock above your bed keep
jerking backward, unraveling your memory,
unticking your thoughts. Each time I speak

to you, you frown and turn to your wife,
asking, *What's happening? What time is it?*
I worry you think I'm our dead mother,

her cold hand patting your arm.
I worry Brother, you'll never know me as me again,
you won't remember that we wouldn't want to live

in a world without each other. If I could pry you
out of this confusion, if I could find someone
strong to carry your body, we could take you home.

I don't want to leave you shivering, but step out
with the family. The doctor points to the blue screen
of your skull, to a gray mass, utters the phrase,

I'm afraid it may be a tumor.
I hate his reverent tone, hate
the unholy noise and disturbance inside

this place, white coats rushing
as if we're the ones in the way. I fear
because he said *tumor* out loud,

that this makes it so. Later in ICU, it is so.
But you know me and grasp my hand.
We talk. But you, whose passion is delivering

the most persuasive closing arguments,
you speak in tongues:
When will my four animals come?

Can we get these sticky bears
off my chest? Doctors have many weapons.
You look at me to see if I understand.

I translate back to you. Your children
will be here tomorrow. These monitors must stay
on your chest. The doctors have a treatment plan.

You nod like a child who is understood.
But in your face is the fear of a man
trying to find his way, a man ripped

from his native land, a man trapped
in a foreign realm that almost mirrors
this one, the fear of a man who grips

a map of old trade routes that lead to a desert tent
of warmed blankets, beeping machines,
and the murmurations of midnight.

Dispatches from the Natural World to My Brother Diagnosed with Glioblastoma

1. Heron

Half-asleep angels softly shaken into this world,
barely contained in their bodies, heads
like duckling fuzz and dizzy, preschoolers toddled
behind their teacher to the gazebo at the town's lake.

A few of the townspeople saw the bird on their morning walk.
A subtle but distinct light emanated from its body, pulsated.

A second sun floated the image of its twin above.
In the shallows, a heron stood on one skinny leg.
The teacher pointed, *great blue heron.*

Neighbors whispered. Their town had suddenly
become magical and terrifying, the kind of place
where no one knew what would happen next.

The heron moved its s-shaped neck and head
side to side. It snatched a fish with its spear-shaped beak,
flipped the fish into its mouth, and swallowed.
Then, the bird with the aura widened its wings,
making slow wing beats to glide
to a tiny island in the middle of the lake.

One child's chest rose as the heron lifted.
He watched its leaving send
concentric waves of circles
across the water.

II. Gravity

Most citizens forgot the heron, remained
tethered to the business of mornings
that pulled them back down like human

kites from the sky. They even forgot
the dreams that occur in the land
of the lucid dreamer, where one

lives inside the dream, and all it takes
to overcome the world is the desire to fly.

III. Gecko

Over coffee and the breaking
of eggs into a bowl, fragments
of night slipped into an older mind.
He remembered last night's dream. Something
had seized his attention, commanded
him to watch it appear
as it shimmied from between two stones,
revealing its identity—of all things, a gecko.
And in the dream he reasoned geckos only bite
when provoked, and bite gently with no
piercing of the skin, no blood.

Sitting down to breakfast, a feeling
of an oncoming message
that he could not stop or control.
Not a praying man per se,
but he believed in signs,
in mystery, and in paying attention.
What did the gecko want? Then a flood

of dispatches from the natural world,
not just a landscape outside himself,
but somehow inside—his lifeblood.
Memories of a beaver cutting
a soundless path through the water,
wood ducks leading a brood
among grasses in the wetland,
the thrum of bullfrogs in the eastern bog,
and the barn owl's screech of dominance
over small creatures. One morning long ago,
a heron searched for prey in the lake.
How the bird glowed. How it made the air
pulse and his body to respond.
For a time, the boy forgot his loneliness.

In last night's dream he had offered an open hand
to the gecko, and the reptile's toes
made his skin tingle as it crept onto his palm.
He had watched its lidless eyes and the black
slits of irises growing almond-shaped
to take in more light. He wanted, no, needed
the gecko to wake him. It wasn't too late.
He needed the gecko to gently gnaw him
alive with its one hundred teeth.

Native Medicine

A shaman tells me to dig
a hole in the ground large enough
for my mouth, to lie belly-down
on the cool earth and to scream
if I need to, scream into the hole
until my voice falls hollow.

I lie down like an animal that does what a man
tells it to do, beside snowflake lichens turned
turquoise on the spruce's sun-rejected slope.
I am not one to sever sleeping tendrils pulsing
in the dirt, not one to worry ants furrowing
under umbrellas of moldy leaves. But I do.

Somewhere, this hole leads to a black sky
above another country, that mirrored city
with church spires, playgrounds,
sidewalks where it is always night.
In that other place, I would never tell
my dying brother to close his eyes, to rest.

Here, in this life, I press my skull to dirt.
Into the hole, at first a whisper,
then finally some primal convulsing,
a sound I've never heard before.
I should have said, *Stay awake and talk
to me. Later, there will be time for sleep.*

Upon Reading That Scientists Have Observed the Golden Ratio in Human Skulls

Consider this—
how everyone's skull
even skulls of the dead—
are perfect containers
with a cranio-ratio
of infinite numbers
like those shared
with pinecones and hurricanes.
The brain's vast potential, a given,
and now its bony shell—
mystery cradling mystery—
a galaxy of one
electrical leap to the next.
Synapses of the stars,
like the night sky above Michelangelo
as he watched a distant lightning storm
across the dark ocean—
intermittent light not audible
where he stood on the beach.
The blinking message
must have made his neck hairs
stand on end.
How is it
that the skull protects
and limits the brain,
but the mind
refuses to be pinned in?
It travels beyond.
Was this the moment

he saw in his mind's eye
the divine fingertip
moving toward his own?
What a wild breakthrough
of the illusion
that he'd ever been in control
of anything.
Like all of us, Brother,
when we learned that inside
your golden skull,
star-shaped cells had grown a tumor
with tentacles fed by your blood.
On the other side of believing
this might be the best thing
that had ever happened to you,
the thing that forced you
to arrive in the present moment
with an endless number
of possibilities,
you fought the one inoperable
conclusion, until your eyes closed.
And the gesture
that took you away—
you raised your arm
to the invisible,
as if to say here I am,
I don't want to go,
but I will.

Second Death

After the first death,
there are others.
Like the morning
I awoke and found
the seasons changed,
I had misplaced spring.
Outside, I saw a smoky
light infected the pines.
Geese startled
over the lake, their wings,
like many hands,
waved goodbye.
Despite my complaints,
bucket men performed
high wire tricks, stunted
the crepe myrtles, maples,
and oaks, lopped off the limbs
that had canopied the street.
And you,
who I could make laugh
just with a silly face,
a Cheshire Cat grin,
you continued
your merry way—dead.
Shade ferns exposed,
hostas slumped with heat.
That crack and the crashing
away from the trunk.

She Addresses Her Brother about Gravity

Today I take the path of hermits
and enter the Sacred Wood of Monteluco.
I hike past the ancient holm oak grove, clutch
your absence up to the bald peak

to spread your ashes. I begin to think of gravity
and its connection to elegy,
the stages of heaviness like the load
on the shoulders of pallbearers, the sinkhole

in the hospital waiting room, the weight
of memory, how it cannot be counted
or contained. And what of the gravity
of your hospice-bed voice when you let me

know for the first time, you, too, had staggered
under the dark power of our childhood?
I shift the heft of your urn. Lighter
in my hand—the remains of dust and bone.

My tight-fisted love cannot give all to air.
Yes, some of it lifts toward St. Peters
in Rome, but too far away. I know
after a time most things settle,

perhaps, almost always, not where
we'd planned for them to land.
I think about the messages I send and receive
back from you, the layers of us, and this new

connection in death, fragile as our childhood
home's fringe tree, each lamplight blossom trapping
the sunset's flame. Here in this place, I question
the small church, how has it managed to kneel

below the clouds for centuries
without blowing away? I try to divine the wrinkles
of the caretaker's face as he walks to the stone barn
where the machinist cuts a sharper edge

for the jangling fall his tools will make.
I plead with the caged—
the pigeons, the penned goats and pigs,
the two truffle-hunting dogs weighed in sleep.

From the kitchen, the clanging of pans,
voices and laughter of women
calling out to each other, their sounds
fading into space. The height of this peak

makes a dizzy view of the fields and distance
of this country I love. Surely here
on the mountaintop that has survived the dead
of winters' ravaging winds? But nothing

in any language answers. Lightheaded, I lean
toward a trance of sun and sky—the thin tether.
Tell me. How much longer
can I keep you earthbound?

The Mouth of the Pelican Is Open

The doorwings of the earth stand open for me.
The mouth of the pelican is opened for me.
The pelican has caused that I shall go forth...
to every place where I wish to go.

—Papyrus of Nu, Egyptian Book of the Dead

I traveled the underworld with you
at dawn, decrypting hieroglyphs,
our safe passage predicted by the pelicans.

You'd been dead a year, and I went to look
for some sign of you. I went to the beach
to gather shells, to the edge where you loved to be.

Did you send these seven-foot wingspans,
these sharp, ravenous beaks on folded necks
from your mirrored world? And just when

I thought the squadron was present, dozens more
flew in and dropped on top of the Gulf.
One relic swooped up and froze mid-air,

a slackened wave stretched. All went silent.
And I believed, in that moment
when the ebb tide halted, on the other side

you'd found fountain pens, Jack Daniels,
the lachrymatory bottle full of mourners' tears.
That huge body began its noisy return

like the flood tide of thought that kept coming.
Soon you'd leave, busy in afterlife,
needled by feelings you had things to do.

I held my breath and watched the bird eye
its prey, crash into the glass sea, into the green
in-between where it seemed we might speak

again, but morning hunted its needs:
the pelican vanished, then reemerged—
its gray throat pouch bulged with a struggling silver.

The angled sun ignited the thrash and swallow
that the pelicans had been dreaming for thirty-six
million years. The frenzy below that burned

without you. The one pelican, now just a pelican,
floated on the ocean with the others, tipped
its head back, opened its mouth for seawater

to spill from both sides, gulped the fish whole.

The Desk

Birds never smash into their reflections.
My breath at the glass wall fogs
the ghostly me standing on air.
For years now, I've come here to lay
my head on your desk's inlaid leather.
I listen for movement of clips and scissors.
I inhale your fountain pen, let the musk of ink
and cologne announce you are here.
The surface sprawls with law books
open at their cracked spines.
Papers in six drawers, papers in stacked files.
What I know is this: You are still dead,
and all I hear is lament cracking,
rising in these cold antique legs.

The Shaman Says Release

I.

I release you, Brother, but only in rations—soft gray
ash on backyard jasmine, a pinch in the Gulf Bay,

a cloudlet that drifts toward Rome. Your remainder
of teeth and bone stay inside the makeshift urn—

stainless steel martini shaker. I never want
to spread your last ashes—you might need them.

You were never one to give up, like that day
in the backyard. I watched you with the half-dead

bush, how you struggled, soft black under your nails,
the dank root ball coming into the light.

I cling to an idea: you are not completely gone.

II.

The shaman takes out his drum.

He sets before me a yarn painting, tells me
to enter it. I want to resist such a silly notion,
but the colors move like sped-up constellations.

I join you in your den. You fool everyone
with the loud Willie Nelson song,
"Nothing I Can Do About It Now."

You wear cowboy boots and a hat
with a wide brim, while inside your brain,
terminal coils tighten their grip.

You hand me a photograph.

Do you remember when we built her,
the peasant snow-woman?
I say yes, though I'd been too young.
You hold the memory alone inside
this long pause. I only hold the photo.
Neither of us remembers who took it.
Our scarves, one tied at her chin, the other
dangling. The two of us looking up
into a distance that seemed endless.

The shaman stops drumming.
The yarn painting is only a yarn painting.

Reprieve

Today, I trust the sun of not knowing
how the noonday cracks
the light on the bush tops, and flint sparks
off the blue bottle tree.
Today, I revel in space around
objects or inside empty vases.
I throw out the old lists, no longer
believe pleasure is the last chore done.
Down the street, a young man praises
his retriever. I admire how they stride
past the just-born hyacinths.
Today, no grave rises to greet me.
I harbor no twisting questions, like:
I know you're gone, but where?
Today, I don't ask why.
I take cues from my cat's thick haunch,
asleep on the porch railing, dust
golden on the ledge, the rusted firepit
beyond. I know you are gone.
I stop holding my breath.

The Shaman

Around the fire, he turns through rising smoke,
jumps the Dance of the Deer. The Shaman circles us.
He waves smoldering sage. Sparks drift on night air—
the ashes of the ancestral dead. Like you,
when you were still alive, he wears a cowboy hat,
but the Shaman's is black, a feather in the band.
I stare into the flames. I fear the blaze will untether
me. He begins to chant, his voice widens the sky
for the stars to appear, dying ones and ones being born.
I'm enthralled, but I don't know if I believe his desire
to heal.

    It's my turn to face the Shaman. In his eyes,
a reverence for wreckage, and my armored heart fears
an upset of time and gravity. I have no need to worship
him, his hair flowing to his waist like an unruly river,
but I do. He pats my shoulders with hawk prayer
feathers, fans my eyelids closed.

           Something slips
inside—vertigo, and I'm not held down by reality.
When the Shaman lays his hand on my arm it feels
delicate but firm, it feels the way a kind person arriving
on the scene of ruins would say—*It's time to go now.*
Here, let me help you walk away.

V

I cannot tell if the day
is ending, or the world, or if
the secret of secrets is inside me again.

—Anna Akhmatova (tr. by Jane Kenyon)

1

Old Prayers

I'm putting all my old prayers in a big box,
no, a lake, or better yet, I'll drop them
like a body from a small boat in the sea,

but not too far out, not in the middle
of the ocean, just under the bridge
where the waves could rock one

to sleep as cars cross back and forth
from the mainland. Old prayers
because they've been around so long,

some would say too long, repeated
to a sky that must hear a sing-song whine.
Large prayers, battered with an aqua green

patina of metal weathervanes, fork
and spoon windchimes. Or maybe the color
of those chalky barnacles that attach

to huge creatures that carry them
wherever they go. And small prayers.
Small as ash or seeds tossed in the fertile

flatlands. Not too close to the tidal creek
that rises to drown all but the tips of reeds,
and then recedes to expose a teeming

mud-glory. The brain should light up
awash with anticipation, replies raining down
hard, sometimes breaching the berm,

flooding the seeds from one location
to another. Which means one could find
an answer when and where you least expect—

in a flaming bush, a look, a book,
a sparrow attacking the glass.
Finally, the bird abandons its rival,

and I settle my body into the warm tub.
I close my eyes and remember that nothing
really bad had happened that Friday the 13th

long ago, when my brother had turned
onto a main street too slowly, and the car
behind us couldn't stop

slamming everything loose forward.
But getting out, we saw not a car,
but a hearse. And the driver yelled,

not in anger, but to check, *Is everybody okay?*
And then, almost singing—*Thank heavens.*
It's our lucky, lucky day.
Just to be alive.

Notes on Poems:

Quote by Edith Södergran (1892-1923) (translated by Stina Katchadourian)—from the anthology *Women in Praise of the Sacred: 43 Centuries of Spiritual Poetry by Women,* edited by Jane Hirshfield. Known for introducing Finland-Swedish modernism, Södergran's poetry did not gain much recognition until after her death. She is now regarded as one of Finland's foremost poets.

"Busboy and Waitress at Everybody's Pizza"—is for Phil and Miranda Paymer. For forty-one years, Everybody's Pizza in Emory Village in Atlanta was a popular hangout for Emory University students, staff, and neighboring residents. The restaurant was famous for its thick-dough pizza, rowdy wait staff, and noisy crowds.

In "Trial Separation," the primate center mentioned refers to the Yerkes National Primate Research Center, renamed Emory National Primate Research Center in Atlanta, Georgia.

"Letter Home" is inspired by the poem "What It Was Like" by Barbara Ras.

"Lessons" is for Elisa Bassetti—Artelingua. The Italian verb "essere" means "to be."

"Before We Are Too Old" refers to the region on the other side of the Milky Way called the Great Attractor. Our galaxy and other nearby galaxies are being pulled toward it. It's been established that the Great Attractor and its nearby galaxies are also moving toward something even larger—a cluster of more than 8000 galaxies with a mass of ten million billion suns.

The quote by Emily Dickinson (1830-1886) is from the book *The Complete Poems of Emily Dickinson,* by Emily Dickinson, Thomas H. Johnson (Editor).

"Matriarch" is for my sister, Katie.

The quote by Adrienne Rich (1929-2012) is from the book *Diving Into the Wreck: Poems 1971-1972.*

"Having Blouses Altered": the phrase "Oh let there be" comes from Richard Wilbur's poem "Love Calls Us to the Things of This World."

"Adoption, Second Day" is dedicated to my son, Zander.

The quote by Kabir (15th century Indian poet) is from the book *Songs of Kabir* by Kabir, translated by Arvind Krishna Mehrotra.

"She Addresses Her Brother About Gravity" refers to the Sacred Wood of Monteluco and the Agriturismo of Bartoli, situated near the town of Spoleto, Italy in Umbria. And is for Daniela Cittadoni.

The quote by Anna Akhmatova (1889-1966, Russian poet) is from the book *The Complete Poems of Anna Akhmatova,* by Anna Akhmatova, Roberta Reeder (Editor), Judith Hemschemeyer (Translator).